Invitation

by Ron DiCianni

with Selected Readings from the
HCSB® New Testament

HOLMAN
CHRISTIAN
STANDARD
B I B L E™

From time to time an artist emerges whose work becomes a touchstone for an entire generation of Christians. In our time, Ron DiCianni has emerged as one of America's best known and most beloved Christian artists. In no other work has such a happy symmetry of spiritual maturity, technical excellence and a passion for the Gospel come to fruition. Reflecting on the deepest needs of the human heart Ron's prayers become tangible in form and color. As one writer put it, "Ron DiCianni is the preacher on Canvas. The theme of his art, like that of any great preacher, always focuses on the cross and redemption. Ron paints and men weep."

The artwork of Ron DiCianni has won him national recognition with many national corporations, including the commission as official artist of the United States Olympic Committee for the Moscow Olympic Games. He has since dedicated his talents solely to the task of proclaiming the "Good News" of the Gospel.

$\mathcal{Y}$ou may be one of the fortunate people in this world having many friends who care about you deeply. Or you may be someone with only a few friends whom you can say really care for you from their hearts.

Whatever the case, I can say with confidence that I know of someone whose love for you far surpasses the love of any friend you've ever known, a love far greater than words can express. Just as this book is someone's gift to you, Jesus showed that love by offering a gift to you to help you understand the most important thing in life.

That person who loves you so overwhelmingly is Jesus Christ, the Son of God. History records the facts of His perfect life and His death by crucifixion, but only the Bible explains the *why*.

That *"why"* is symbolically illustrated in this painting. We see the piercing nail that fastened the feet of Jesus to the cross, reminding us of other nails that pierced His outstretched arms so that His entire body writhed in that agony.

But it was not really those nails that kept Him on the cross. What held Him there was His incomparable love, a love stronger than His will to live, stronger than His desire to call ten thousand angels to His rescue. Stronger than any longing to escape this most inhumane form of execution.

Let me explain. As you see, this painting is about the person responsible for driving those nails. He is responsible, and so are you. That's why the hammer and the nails are in the hands of the man kneeling at the foot of the cross.

How are we responsible?

Jesus died because God, in giving His perfectly innocent Son to death, was paying the penalty of what the Bible calls our sin—your sin, and mine. What is sin, and why should it warrant such a horrible penalty?

WRONG CHOICES

I'm sure you'll agree that at some point in your life you've made wrong choices. Perhaps at times you've been dishonest toward someone in order to further your own interests. Or you may have spoken hateful or belittling words to others, or caused someone hurt by your actions, or had immoral thoughts of one sort or another. Whatever these wrong choices, you thereby transgressed a higher law than any country's judicial system.

These wrong choices are what the Bible means by "sin." At times you may have thought these mistakes were minor enough to go unseen by God, or were long ago forgotten. But that cannot be. The Bible expresses the magnitude of even the smallest sin:

> *For whoever keeps the entire law, yet fails in one point, is guilty of breaking it all.*
>
> *James 2:10*

With every sinful choice we therefore cause great offense to God our Creator, who is holy and righteous. In His own unchanging perfection, He cannot accept us in such a sinful condition. He would not be holy and righteous and perfect if He did.

Furthermore, our sinful condition is something we have no way of getting rid of on our own. Once we sin the first time, it's part of us, no matter how small or insignificant we may consider our wrong choice.

No amount of our good deeds can be "good" enough, even if we've attended church every day of our lives, given every dollar we've ever made to charity, and rescued dozens of people from burning buildings. As those who have sinned, we are utterly lost as far as God's heaven and eternal life are concerned. We have broken God's Commandments, and there's nothing we can do to make up for it, however harsh that may seem.

The awful result is a permanent separation between us and God. It's a wall so thick that dynamite couldn't flake off one chip of it to get us closer to God, who knows absolutely everything about us and about our past.

FACTS OF THE MATTER

These are uncomfortable facts to think about, which is why so many people try not to. But the full truth will be inescapable when we die. Just imagine what that wall of separation from God will mean when we face His irreversible verdict as to where we will spend eternity—either with God in His heaven, where life is truly life, or shut out from His loving presence forever. There are no second chances, no second opinions.

Perhaps you've already given thought to that. After you die, where do you plan to spend eternity, and with whom? And what can you offer the "gatekeeper" as admission to the place where you want to go?

Some people tell themselves, *I can worry about that later*, or, *Somehow everything will take care of itself in the end.* Unfortunately, while such blind hope or wishful thinking may seem comforting for now, it will not be of any real value when we die.

Others conclude, *It doesn't matter anyway, because all roads lead to the same place.* Or, *This life is really all there is.* Or even, *If there is a God, He's too good to send anyone to hell.* But such sentiments directly contradict what God Himself has made clear in the Bible.

Others have thought, *God, even if You exist and even if You did all that the Bible says You did for me, I'd rather take my chances based on my own abilities and power. I don't need Your help, and I certainly don't need You to tell me how to live.* They may not verbalize this attitude quite so bluntly, but in effect they may as well have.

Still others assume that God "owes them something" simply by virtue of their existence here in His universe— while forgetting that we all owe Him for every breath we take and every beat of our heart.

People are always coming up with such arguments and excuses in their uneasiness with the facts of the matter as explained in the Bible. But the truth is that we, as sinners, must appear before God when we die, and there's nothing you or I or anyone could offer as admission into His heaven, nothing we can pay to cover the price required for our own sin.

PROOF OF HIS LOVE

There is only one payment God will accept: the death of Jesus, His perfect and sinless Son. This is a critical point the Bible makes in directing us to Jesus:

> *There is salvation in no one else, for there is no other name under heaven given to people by which we must be saved.* *Acts 4:12*

This passage mentions "salvation," because through the love of Jesus it is indeed possible to be saved from having to spend eternity away from God as the consequence for our sin. Love caused Jesus to take on the penalty for all our sins—past, present, and future—so we could stand sinless and blameless before God.

That's what made the death of Jesus so agonizing for Him. Carrying that multitude of sins was something only He, in his perfection, could do. And He did it. What greater proof could there be of His love?

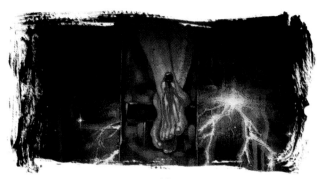

The wonderful truth of all this is summed up in one of the best-known statements in the Bible, a declaration that also reveals our proper response:

For God loved the world in this way: He gave His only Son, so that everyone who believes in Him will not perish but have eternal life. John 3:16

It's by believing in Jesus that we escape being condemned to hell and instead are allowed to enjoy eternal life in heaven. The Bible calls this the "Good News" (that's what the word *gospel* means). And indeed such a plan for our salvation, springing from such unfathomable love, is so wonderful as to be beyond human comprehension, isn't it?

Yet instead of responding to this Good News with faith—by repenting of our sin and gratefully accepting our salvation in Jesus—so many people ignore it or even skeptically thumb their nose in God's face. They need to be reminded of a young man we often call "the prodigal son" in a story Jesus told, a story most of us can identify with in some way.

This young man left his father and his home to seek greener pastures, only to squander all he had in reckless living. Humiliated and ashamed, he finally came to his senses and decided to return home. He rehearsed the sincere words he would use with his father to acknowledge his own sin and his unworthiness to ever again be treated as his father's son.

The story's incredible climax is portrayed in this painting. Instead of facing the father's wrath, the son did not even make it all the way home before his father came running out to meet him with open arms and tender forgiveness. He had been waiting the whole time for his son's return.

This is a great way to picture God. He not only knows that you've left home, but eagerly expects and looks for your return. He is not waiting to punish, but to restore.

For us, Jesus—because of all that he has done for us in his great love for us—is our own way back home, our only path to eternal life in a journey that can truly be an adventure in every aspect. As Jesus Himself said,

> *"I am the way, the truth, and the life. No one comes to the Father except through Me."*   *John 14:6*

Believing in Jesus means so much more than just a mental agreement with the fact that He died for you. It means turning over every aspect of your life to Him, abandoning your own resources and even the very ownership of yourself and placing all of that into the hands of Jesus, your guide on this journey. You choose to depend on His resources rather than your own. You follow His lead, with complete recognition of His ability and authority to guide you to the end and beyond. You walk by His rules, with total faith in His leadership. Along the way you learn servanthood, humility, and even suffering as you discover how to submit and yield to your Guide.

PROOF OF HIS POWER

But how can we know for sure that Jesus can do all this? How do we know He's truly our way home, our trustworthy Guide?

To give us the greatest possible proof that His death opened up for us the way into eternal life, Jesus did the impossible: He rose up from the dead.

The resurrection of Jesus Christ is more than historical fact. It is the defining difference between Christianity and all other religions, philosophies, and ideas. The bodies of the great leaders of the past, in every field or endeavor, are lying in their graves with a marker signifying their importance. But at the tomb of Jesus Christ there's no need for a marker–because He's not there. Hundreds saw Him bodily after His resurrection. He had conquered death, just as He said He would.

This painting signifies what the moment might have been like when Christ came back to life and the stone at the entrance to His tomb was about to roll back—not to let Him out, but to let others see in—into the tomb's emptiness, the confirmation that Jesus had indeed accomplished what He set out to do. What greater proof could He offer of His power to do all things?

BEING READY

If you have not already decided to receive the gift of salvation and eternal life which Jesus offers you and to follow Him as your only Guide on your journey toward eternity, then in light of His incomparable love as seen in His death on the cross and His incomparable power as seen in His resurrection, can there really be any valid reason why you should not make that decision right now?

If you agree that indeed there is no valid reason, are you ready to recognize that you are a sinner, and that Jesus is your only hope of having your sin wiped away in the sight of our Holy God? Are you ready to receive God's offer of eternal life on His terms and His alone? Are you ready to recognize that your life no longer belongs to you but to Jesus, and to allow Him to take your place as the owner and manager of your life?

If you are ready, then think back again to the story Jesus told of the prodigal son. There finally came a moment in time when the young man came to his senses. He fully recognized and acknowledged the wrongness of his sinful ways, which is something we also must do. This is called confession, which simply means recognizing and acknowledging our sin before God, and agreeing with God that we've been going the wrong way.

Remember too in Jesus' story how the young man, after reaching that point in his understanding, responded with absolute decisiveness. He chose at once to leave his sinful ways behind and to instead set out toward home.

That decisive turnaround in his life is what is known as repentance; this, too, is a step we also need to take in turning to Jesus. As Jesus Himself expressed it in the Bible,

No, I tell you; but unless you repent, you will all perish as well! Luke 13:3

Repentance is simply the acknowledgment that we have sinned, and that we commit to following God's way through Jesus instead of our own way. Repentance is what we do in response to what Jesus did. It's our only fitting response to the mercy God has shown us in paying the full penalty for our sin.

A helpful way of realizing this is to consider an incident recorded in the Bible. Some religious leaders had dragged before Jesus a woman caught in the act of adultery. Their laws called for her to be stoned to death, but Jesus put an end to that by saying to them,

"The one without sin among you should be the first to throw a stone at her." John 8:7

As the woman's accusers drifted away one by one, Jesus did something even better for her: He told her that He Himself did not condemn her.

After extending such mercy, Jesus then added—in words meant for you and me as well as for her—

"Go, and from now on do not sin any more."
John 8:11

It is that moment, when he said those words, that defines this painting. Just as Jesus extended His hand of mercy to this woman, so God lovingly extends His hand of mercy to you, along with a command to turn away from your sin.

After confession and repentance, the final aspect of your decision is to personally accept the gift of salvation that God offers each of us. It is just like the prodigal son's acceptance of his father's embrace and forgiveness and restoration.

You can dedicate this decision directly to God by praying a prayer that expresses your confession, your repentance and your acceptance of his gift. When I prayed that prayer years ago, I said something like this:

Jesus, I repent of having broken God's law by my sins. I ask Your forgiveness,

and pray that You will come and take
ownership of my life, now and forever.
Please come into my heart and occupy
the place of authority over my life.
I accept Your death as my only means of
salvation, and I intend to follow You from this
day forward, not worrying what it may cost me.
I invite You into my heart, and I count on
You to never leave me or forsake me. Thank
You for saving me now. I love You. Amen.

You may have a more eloquent prayer than that, or a longer prayer, but all that matters is that the words are from your heart.

As you sincerely pray these things before God, then in God's eyes your life is now "in Christ." And the Bible says,

Therefore if anyone
is in Christ, there is
a new creation; old
things have passed
away, and look, new
things have come.
2 Cor. 5:17

Now What?

If you have prayed this prayer of salvation, I offer you my congratulations. You are now a Christian! Welcome to the family of God! You have chosen wisely, because those who reject God's truth and His offer of love in Jesus cannot escape God's judgment and the penalty of being excluded from His presence in eternity.

A minister of the gospel once put it like this:

In the moral conflict now raging around us, whoever is on God's side is on the winning side and cannot lose; whoever is on the other side is on the losing side and cannot win. Here there is no chance, no gamble. There is freedom to choose which side we shall be on, but no freedom to negotiate the results of the choice once it is made.

By choosing to accept God's invitation, you are now on the winning side and cannot lose. And your decision is vastly more than just an end to your old life; it is the beginning of a brand new one.

Jesus talked about two roads. One is the "broad road," leading to destruction. That's the one you were on before. But now you are taking the other road, the road that leads to your true home and true fulfillment—and the one Jesus called the "narrow road." *(Incidentally, He said that few people ever find this road. How privileged you are to be one of those few!)*

Along this road you will learn how to live the Christian life effectively as you pray, read the Bible, and get to know other Christians who can help you. And on that road you will find all you've ever longed for, and so much more, all as a result of God's mercy. His mercy was there for you in sending Jesus His Son to die for you, but that wasn't the end of it. His mercy never stops flowing toward His children in new ways day after day as they travel on the road to eternity.

And even greater than these joys along the road will be the higher blessing God invites us to, a blessing depicted in this final painting. The moment you leave this world, you can be certain that there will be a Savior waiting with open arms for you, to welcome you safely home.

Above all else, His invitation is the invitation to enjoy him forever.

The following assortment of selected passages from the Bible explains the miracle of salvation. It's the story of how God meets people every day who are lost on the road of life—(and getting farther away from home all the time)—and how He wipes away every obstacle that keeps them from living in perfect peace with Him. Hear His voice as you read. He's calling you back. Calling you higher. Calling you home.

THE REASON JESUS CAME

First and Foremost
John, chapter 1

¹ In the beginning was the Word;
and the Word was with God,
and the Word was God.
² He was with God in the beginning.
³ All things were created through Him,
and apart from Him not one thing was created
that has been created.
⁴ In Him was life,
and that life was the light of men.
⁵ That light shines in the darkness,
yet the darkness did not overcome it.
⁶ There was a man named John
who was sent from God.
⁷ He came as a witness
to testify about the light,

so that all might believe through him.

8 He was not the light,

but he came to testify about the light.

9 The true light, who gives light to everyone,

was coming into the world.

10 He was in the world,

and the world was created through Him,

yet the world did not know Him.

11 He came to His own,

and His own people did not receive Him.

12 But to all who did receive Him,

He gave them the right to be children of God,

to those who believe in His name,

13 who were born,

not of blood,

or of the will of the flesh,

or of the will of man,

but of God.

14 The Word became flesh

and took up residence among us.

We observed His glory,

the glory as the only Son from the Father,

full of grace and truth.

15 (John testified concerning Him and exclaimed,

"This was the One of whom I said,

'The One coming after me has surpassed me,

because He existed before me.' ")

16 For we have all received grace after grace

from His fullness.

17 For the law was given through Moses;

grace and truth came through Jesus Christ.

18 No one has ever seen God.
The only Son—
the One who is at the Father's side—
He has revealed Him.

We Must Be Born Again
John, chapter 3

1 There was a man from the Pharisees named Nicodemus, a ruler of the Jews. 2 This man came to Him at night and said, "Rabbi, we know that You have come from God as a teacher, for no one could perform these signs You do unless God were with him."

3 Jesus replied, "I assure you: Unless someone is born again, he cannot see the kingdom of God."

4 "But how can anyone be born when he is old?" Nicodemus asked Him. "Can he enter his mother's womb a second time and be born?"

5 Jesus answered, "I assure you: Unless someone is born of water and the Spirit, he cannot enter the kingdom of God. 6 Whatever is born of the flesh is flesh, and whatever is born of the Spirit is spirit. 7 Do not be amazed that I told you that you must be born again. 8 The wind blows where it pleases, and you hear its sound, but you don't know where it comes from or where it is going. So it is with everyone born of the Spirit."

9 "How can these things be?" asked Nicodemus.

10 "Are you a teacher of Israel and don't know these things?" Jesus replied. 11 "I assure you: We speak what We

know and We testify to what We have seen, but you do not accept Our testimony. 12 If I have told you about things that happen on earth and you don't believe, how will you believe if I tell you about things of heaven? 13 No one has ascended into heaven except the One who descended from heaven—the Son of Man. 14 Just as Moses lifted up the serpent in the wilderness, so the Son of Man must be lifted up, 15 so that everyone who believes in Him will have eternal life.

16 "For God loved the world in this way: He gave His only Son, so that everyone who believes in Him will not perish but have eternal life. 17 For God did not send His Son into the world that He might judge the world, but that the world might be saved through Him. 18 Anyone who believes in Him is not judged, but anyone who does not believe is already judged, because he has not believed in the name of the only Son of God.

19 "This, then, is the judgment: the light has come into the world, and people loved darkness rather than the light because their deeds were evil. 20 For everyone who practices wicked things hates the light and avoids it, so that his deeds may not be exposed. 21 But anyone who lives by the truth comes to the light, so that his works may be shown to be accomplished by God."

He Offers Us Eternal Life
John, chapter 6

28 "What can we do to perform the works of God?" they asked.

29 Jesus replied, "This is the work of God: that you believe in the One He has sent."

[30] "Then what sign are You going to do so we may see and believe You?" they asked. "What are You going to perform? [31] Our fathers ate the manna in the desert, just as it is written: 'He gave them bread from heaven to eat.' "

[32] Jesus said to them, "I assure you: Moses didn't give you the bread from heaven, but My Father gives you the true bread from heaven. [33] For the bread of God is the One who comes down from heaven and gives life to the world."

[34] Then they said, "Sir, give us this bread always!"

[35] "I am the bread of life," Jesus told them. "No one who comes to Me will ever be hungry, and no one who believes in Me will ever be thirsty again. [36] But as I told you, you've seen Me, and yet you do not believe. [37] Everyone the Father gives Me will come to Me, and the one who comes to Me I will never cast out. [38] For I have come down from heaven, not to do My will, but the will of Him who sent Me. [39] This is the will of Him who sent Me: that I should lose none of those He has given Me but should raise them up on the last day. [40] For this is the will of My Father: that everyone who sees the Son and believes in Him may have eternal life, and I will raise him up on the last day."

[41] Therefore the Jews started complaining about Him, because He said, "I am the bread that came down from heaven." [42] They were saying, "Isn't this Jesus the son of Joseph, whose father and mother we know? How can He now say, 'I have come down from heaven'?"

[43] Jesus answered them, "Stop complaining among yourselves. [44] No one can come to Me unless the Father who sent Me draws him, and I will raise him up on the last day. [45] It is written in the Prophets: 'And they will all be

taught by God.' Everyone who has listened to and learned from the Father comes to Me— 46 not that anyone has seen the Father except the One who is from God. He has seen the Father.

47 "I assure you: Anyone who believes has eternal life. 48 I am the bread of life. 49 Your fathers ate the manna in the desert, and they died. 50 This is the bread that comes down from heaven so that anyone may eat of it and not die. 51 I am the living bread that came down from heaven. If anyone eats of this bread he will live forever. The bread that I will give for the life of the world is My flesh."

52 At that, the Jews argued among themselves, "How can this man give us His flesh to eat?"

53 So Jesus said to them, "I assure you: Unless you eat the flesh of the Son of Man and drink His blood, you do not have life in yourselves. 54 Anyone who eats My flesh and drinks My blood has eternal life, and I will raise him up on the last day, 55 because My flesh is true food and My blood is true drink. 56 The one who eats My flesh and drinks My blood lives in Me, and I in him. 57 Just as the living Father sent Me and I live because of the Father, so the one who feeds on Me will live because of Me. 58 This is the bread that came down from heaven; it is not like the manna your fathers ate—and they died.

The one who eats this bread will live forever."

Where Else Can We Go?
John, chapter 6

60 Therefore, when many of His disciples heard this, they said, "This teaching is hard! Who can accept it?"

⁶¹ Jesus, knowing in Himself that His disciples were complaining about this, asked them, "Does this offend you? ⁶² Then what if you were to observe the Son of Man ascending to where He was before? ⁶³ The Spirit is the One who gives life. The flesh doesn't help at all. The words that I have spoken to you are spirit and are life. ⁶⁴ But there are some among you who don't believe." (For Jesus knew from the beginning those who would not believe and the one who would betray Him.) ⁶⁵ He said, "This is why I told you that no one can come to Me unless it is granted to him by the Father."

⁶⁶ From that moment many of His disciples turned back and no longer walked with Him. ⁶⁷ Therefore Jesus said to the Twelve, "You don't want to go away too, do you?"

⁶⁸ Simon Peter answered, "Lord, to whom should we go? You have the words of eternal life. ⁶⁹ And we have come to believe and know that You are the Holy One of God!"

Here Are Our Two Choices
Matthew, chapter 7

²⁴ "Therefore, everyone who hears these words of Mine and acts on them will be like a sensible man who built his house on the rock. ²⁵ The rain fell, the rivers rose, and the winds blew and pounded that house. Yet it didn't collapse, because its foundation was on the rock. ²⁶ But everyone who hears these words of Mine and doesn't act on them will be like a foolish man who built his house on the sand. ²⁷ The rain fell, the rivers rose, the winds blew and pounded that house, and it collapsed. And its collapse was great!"

HE SEEKS THOSE
WHO ARE LOST

Jesus' Parables of the Lost Sheep and the Lost Coin
Luke, chapter 15

4 "What man among you, who has 100 sheep and loses one of them, does not leave the 99 in the open field and go after the lost one until he finds it? 5 When he has found it, he joyfully puts it on his shoulders, 6 and coming home, he calls his friends and neighbors together, saying to them, 'Rejoice with me, because I have found my lost sheep!' 7 I tell you, in the same way, there will be more joy in heaven over one sinner who repents than over 99 righteous people who don't need repentance.

8 "Or what woman who has 10 silver coins, if she loses one coin, does not light a lamp, sweep the house, and search carefully until she finds it? 9 When she finds it, she calls her

women friends and neighbors together, saying, 'Rejoice with me, because I have found the silver coin I lost!' 10 I tell you, in the same way, there is joy in the presence of God's angels over one sinner who repents."

Jesus' Parable of the Lost Son
Luke, chapter 15

11 He also said: "A man had two sons. 12 The younger of them said to his father, 'Father, give me the share of the estate I have coming to me.' So he distributed the assets to them. 13 Not many days later, the younger son gathered together all he had and traveled to a distant country, where he squandered his estate in foolish living. 14 After he had spent everything, a severe famine struck that country, and he had nothing. 15 Then he went to work for one of the citizens of that country, who sent him into his fields to feed pigs. 16 He longed to eat his fill from the carob pods the pigs were eating, and no one would give him any. 17 But when he came to his senses, he said, 'How many of my father's hired hands have more than enough food, and here I am dying of hunger! 18 I'll get up, go to my father, and say to him, "Father, I have sinned against heaven and in your sight. 19 I'm no longer worthy to be called your son. Make me like one of your hired hands." ' 20 So he got up and went to his father. But while the son was still a long way off, his father saw him and was filled with compassion. He ran, threw his arms around his neck, and kissed him. 21 The son said to him, 'Father, I have sinned against heaven and in your sight. I'm no longer worthy to be called your son.'

22 "But the father told his slaves, 'Quick! Bring out the best robe and put it on him; put a ring on his finger and sandals on his feet. 23 Then bring the fattened calf and slaughter it, and let's celebrate with a feast, 24 because this son of mine was dead and is alive again; he was lost and is found!' So they began to celebrate.

25 "Now his older son was in the field; as he came near the house, he heard music and dancing. 26 So he summoned one of the servants and asked what these things meant. 27 'Your brother is here,' he told him, 'and your father has slaughtered the fattened calf because he has him back safe and sound.'

28 "Then he became angry and didn't want to go in. So his father came out and pleaded with him. 29 But he replied to his father, 'Look, I have been slaving many years for you, and I have never disobeyed your orders; yet you never gave me a young goat so I could celebrate with my friends. 30 But when this son of yours came, who has devoured your assets with prostitutes, you slaughtered the fattened calf for him.'

31 " 'Son,' he said to him, 'you are always with me, and everything I have is yours. 32 But we had to celebrate and rejoice, because this brother of yours was dead and is alive again; he was lost and is found.' "

This Is the Only Way
John, chapter 14

1 "Your heart must not be troubled. Believe in God; believe also in Me. 2 In My Father's house are many dwelling places; if not, I would have told you. I am going

away to prepare a place for you. 3 If I go away and prepare a place for you, I will come back and receive you to Myself, so that where I am you may be also. 4 You know the way where I am going."

5 "Lord," Thomas said, "we don't know where You're going. How can we know the way?"

6 Jesus told him, "I am the way, the truth, and the life. No one comes to the Father except through Me.

Jesus Wants to Come to Stay
John, chapter 14

19 "In a little while the world will see Me no longer, but you will see Me. Because I live, you will live too. 20 In that day you will know that I am in My Father, you are in Me, and I am in you. 21 The one who has My commandments and keeps them is the one who loves Me. And the one who loves Me will be loved by My Father. I also will love him and will reveal Myself to him."

22 Judas (not Iscariot) said to Him, "Lord, how is it You're going to reveal Yourself to us and not to the world?"

23 Jesus answered, "If anyone loves Me, he will keep My word. My Father will love him, and We will come to him and make Our home with him. 24 The one who doesn't love Me will not keep My words. The word that you hear is not Mine, but is from the Father who sent Me.

25 "I have spoken these things to you while I remain with you. 26 But the Counselor, the Holy Spirit, whom the Father will send in My name, will teach you all things and remind you of everything I have told you.

HIS ANSWER TO OUR PROBLEM

Look at All We've Been Promised
Ephesians, chapter 1

3 Blessed be the God and Father of our Lord Jesus Christ, who has blessed us with every spiritual blessing in the heavens, in Christ; 4 for He chose us in Him, before the foundation of the world, to be holy and blameless in His sight. In love 5 He predestined us to be adopted through Jesus Christ for Himself, according to His favor and will, 6 to the praise of His glorious grace that He favored us with in the Beloved.

7 In Him we have redemption through His blood, the forgiveness of our trespasses, according to the riches of His grace 8 that He lavished on us with all wisdom and understanding. 9 He made known to us the mystery of His will, according to His good pleasure that He planned in Him 10 for the administration of the days of fulfillment—to bring

everything together in the Messiah, both things in heaven and things on earth in Him.

¹¹ In Him we were also made His inheritance, predestined according to the purpose of the One who works out everything in agreement with the decision of His will, ¹² so that we who had already put our hope in the Messiah might bring praise to His glory.

¹³ In Him you also, when you heard the word of truth, the gospel of your salvation—in Him when you believed—were sealed with the promised Holy Spirit. ¹⁴ He is the down payment of our inheritance, for the redemption of the possession, to the praise of His glory.

But We Are Hopeless without Christ
Titus, chapter 3

³ For we too were once foolish, disobedient, deceived, captives of various passions and pleasures, living in malice and envy, hateful, detesting one another.
⁴ But when the goodness and love for man
appeared from God our Savior,
⁵ He saved us—
not by works of righteousness that we had done,
but according to His mercy,
through the washing of regeneration
and renewal by the Holy Spirit.
⁶ This Spirit He poured out on us abundantly
through Jesus Christ our Savior,
⁷ so that having been justified by His grace,
we may become heirs with the hope of eternal life.

Only He Can Take Us from Death to Life
Ephesians, chapter 2

¹ And you were dead in your trespasses and sins ² in which you previously walked according to this worldly age, according to the ruler of the atmospheric domain, the spirit now working in the disobedient. ³ We too all previously lived among them in our fleshly desires, carrying out the inclinations of our flesh and thoughts, and by nature we were children under wrath, as the others were also. ⁴ But God, who is abundant in mercy, because of His great love that He had for us, ⁵ made us alive with the Messiah even though we were dead in trespasses. By grace you are saved! ⁶ He also raised us up with Him and seated us with Him in the heavens, in Christ Jesus, ⁷ so that in the coming ages He might display the immeasurable riches of His grace in His kindness to us in Christ Jesus. ⁸ For by grace you are saved through faith, and this is not from yourselves; it is God's gift— ⁹ not from works, so that no one can boast. ¹⁰ For we are His making, created in Christ Jesus for good works, which God prepared ahead of time so that we should walk in them.

Only He Can Give Us Peace with God
Romans, chapter 5

¹ Therefore, since we have been declared righteous by faith, we have peace with God through our Lord Jesus Christ. ² Also through Him, we have obtained access by faith into this grace in which we stand, and we rejoice in

the hope of the glory of God. 3 And not only that, but we also rejoice in our afflictions, because we know that affliction produces endurance, 4 endurance produces proven character, and proven character produces hope. 5 This hope does not disappoint, because God's love has been poured out in our hearts through the Holy Spirit who was given to us.

Only He Can Declare Us Righteous in God's Sight
Romans, chapter 5

6 For while we were still helpless, at the appointed moment, Christ died for the ungodly. 7 For rarely will someone die for a just person—though for a good person perhaps someone might even dare to die. 8 But God proves His own love for us in that while we were still sinners Christ died for us! 9 Much more then, since we have now been declared righteous by His blood, we will be saved through Him from wrath. 10 For if, while we were enemies, we were reconciled to God through the death of His Son, then how much more, having been reconciled, will we be saved by His life! 11 And not only that, but we also rejoice in God through our Lord Jesus Christ, through whom we have now received reconciliation.

His Grace Is Our Only Chance
Romans, chapter 5

12 Therefore, just as sin entered the world through one man, and death through sin, in this way death spread to all

men, because all sinned. 13 In fact, sin was in the world before the law, but sin is not charged to one's account when there is no law. 14 Nevertheless, death reigned from Adam to Moses, even over those who did not sin in the likeness of Adam's transgression. He is a prototype of the Coming One.

15 But the gift is not like the trespass. For if by the one man's trespass the many died, how much more have the grace of God and the gift overflowed to the many by the grace of the one man, Jesus Christ. 16 And the gift is not like the one man's sin, because from one sin came the judgment, resulting in condemnation, but from many trespasses came the gift, resulting in justification. 17 Since by the one man's trespass, death reigned through that one man, how much more will those who receive the overflow of grace and the gift of righteousness reign in life through the one man, Jesus Christ.

18 So then, as through one trespass there is condemnation for everyone, so also through one righteous act there is life-giving justification for everyone. 19 For just as through one man's disobedience the many were made sinners, so also through the one man's obedience the many will be made righteous. 20 The law came along to multiply the trespass. But where sin multiplied, grace multiplied even more, 21 so that, just as sin reigned in death, so also grace will reign through righteousness, resulting in eternal life through Jesus Christ our Lord.

THINK ABOUT IT

What If You Were Free from Sin?
Romans, chapter 6

¹ What should we say then? Should we continue in sin in order that grace may multiply? ² Absolutely not! How can we who died to sin still live in it? ³ Or are you unaware that all of us who were baptized into Christ Jesus were baptized into His death? ⁴ Therefore we were buried with Him by baptism into death, in order that, just as Christ was raised from the dead by the glory of the Father, so we too may walk in a new way of life. ⁵ For if we have been joined with Him in the likeness of His death, we will certainly also be in the likeness of His resurrection. ⁶ For we know that our old self was crucified with Him in order that sin's dominion over the body may be abolished, so that we may no longer be enslaved to sin, ⁷ since a person who has died is freed from sin's claims. ⁸ Now if we died with Christ, we believe that we will also

live with Him, 9 because we know that Christ, having been raised from the dead, no longer dies. Death no longer rules over Him. 10 For in that He died, He died to sin once for all; but in that He lives, He lives to God. 11 So, you too consider yourselves dead to sin, but alive to God in Christ Jesus.

12 Therefore do not let sin reign in your mortal body, so that you obey its desires. 13 And do not offer any parts of it to sin as weapons for unrighteousness. But as those who are alive from the dead, offer yourselves to God, and all the parts of yourselves to God as weapons for righteousness. 14 For sin will not rule over you, because you are not under law but under grace.

What If God Wiped Your Slate Totally Clean?
Romans, chapter 6

15 What then? Should we sin because we are not under law but under grace? Absolutely not! 16 Do you not know that if you offer yourselves to someone as obedient slaves, you are slaves of that one you obey—either of sin leading to death or of obedience leading to righteousness? 17 But thank God that, although you used to be slaves of sin, you obeyed from the heart that pattern of teaching you were entrusted to, 18 and having been liberated from sin, you became enslaved to righteousness. 19 I am using a human analogy because of the weakness of your flesh. For just as you offered the parts of yourselves as slaves to moral impurity, and to greater and greater lawlessness, so now offer them as slaves to righteousness, which results in sanctification. 20 For when you were slaves of sin, you were free from

allegiance to righteousness. 21 And what fruit was produced then from the things you are now ashamed of? For the end of those things is death. 22 But now, since you have been liberated from sin and become enslaved to God, you have your fruit, which results in sanctification—and the end is eternal life! 23 For the wages of sin is death, but the gift of God is eternal life in Christ Jesus our Lord.

You Could Live without a Minute's Worry
Romans, chapter 8

1 Therefore, no condemnation now exists for those in Christ Jesus, 2 because the Spirit's law of life in Christ Jesus has set you free from the law of sin and of death. 3 What the law could not do since it was limited by the flesh, God did. He condemned sin in the flesh by sending His own Son in flesh like ours under sin's domain, and as a sin offering, 4 in order that the law's requirement would be accomplished in us who do not walk according to the flesh but according to the Spirit. 5 For those whose lives are according to the flesh think about the things of the flesh, but those whose lives are according to the Spirit, about the things of the Spirit. 6 For the mind-set of the flesh is death, but the mind-set of the Spirit is life and peace. 7 For the mind-set of the flesh is hostile to God because it does not submit itself to God's law, for it is unable to do so. 8 Those whose lives are in the flesh are unable to please God. 9 You, however, are not in the flesh, but in the Spirit, since the Spirit of God lives in you. But if anyone does not have the Spirit of Christ, he does not belong to Him. 10 Now if Christ is in you, the body is dead because of sin, but

the Spirit is life because of righteousness. [11] And if the Spirit of Him who raised Jesus from the dead lives in you, then He who raised Christ from the dead will also bring your mortal bodies to life through His Spirit who lives in you.

You Could Enjoy a True Relationship with God
Romans, chapter 8

[12] So then, brothers, we are not obligated to the flesh to live according to the flesh, [13] for if you live according to the flesh, you are going to die. But if by the Spirit you put to death the deeds of the body, you will live. [14] All those led by God's Spirit are God's sons. [15] For you did not receive a spirit of slavery to fall back into fear, but you received the Spirit of adoption, by whom we cry out, "*Abba*, Father!" [16] The Spirit Himself testifies together with our spirit that we are God's children, [17] and if children, also heirs—heirs of God and co-heirs with Christ—seeing that we suffer with Him so that we may also be glorified with Him.

You Could Always Know that God Was in Control
Romans, chapter 8

[18] For I consider that the sufferings of this present time are not worth comparing with the glory that is going to be revealed to us. [19] For the creation eagerly waits with antic-ipation for God's sons to be revealed. [20] For the creation was subjected to futility—not willingly, but because of Him who subjected it—in the hope [21] that the creation itself will also

be set free from the bondage of corruption into the glorious freedom of God's children. 22 For we know that the whole creation has been groaning together with labor pains until now. 23 And not only that, but we ourselves who have the Spirit as the firstfruits—we also groan within ourselves, eagerly waiting for adoption, the redemption of our bodies. 24 Now in this hope we were saved, yet hope that is seen is not hope, because who hopes for what he sees? 25 But if we hope for what we do not see, we eagerly wait for it with patience.

26 In the same way the Spirit also joins to help in our weakness, because we do not know what to pray for as we should, but the Spirit Himself intercedes for us with unspoken groanings. 27 And He who searches the hearts knows the Spirit's mind-set, because He intercedes for the saints according to the will of God.

28 We know that all things work together for the good of those who love God: those who are called according to His purpose. 29 For those He foreknew He also predestined to be conformed to the image of His Son, so that He would be the firstborn among many brothers. 30 And those He predestined, He also called; and those He called, He also justified; and those He justified, He also glorified.

You Could Look Forward to Forever
Romans, chapter 8

31 What then are we to say about these things?
If God is for us, who is against us?
32 He did not even spare His own Son,

but offered Him up for us all;
how will He not also with Him grant us everything?
33 Who can bring an accusation against God's elect?
God is the One who justifies.
34 Who is the one who condemns?
Christ Jesus is the One who died,
but even more, has been raised;
He also is at the right hand of God and intercedes for us.
35 Who can separate us from the love of Christ?
Can affliction or anguish or persecution
or famine or nakedness or danger or sword?
36 As it is written:
"Because of You we are being put to death all day long;
we are counted as sheep to be slaughtered."
37 No, in all these things we are more than victorious
through Him who loved us.
38 For I am persuaded that neither death nor life,
nor angels nor rulers,
nor things present, nor things to come, nor powers,
39 nor height, nor depth, nor any other created thing
will have the power to separate us
from the love of God that is in Christ Jesus our Lord!

WHAT'S STOPPING YOU?

He Has Already Come to You
Ephesians, chapter 2

11 So then, remember that at one time you were Gentiles in the flesh—called "the uncircumcised" by those called "the circumcised," done by hand in the flesh. 12 At that time you were without the Messiah, excluded from the citizenship of Israel, and foreigners to the covenants of the promise, with no hope and without God in the world. 13 But now in Christ Jesus, you who were far away have been brought near by the blood of the Messiah. 14 For He is our peace, who made both groups one and tore down the dividing wall of hostility. In His flesh, 15 He did away with the law of the commandments in regulations, so that He might create in Himself one new man from the two, resulting in peace. 16 He did this so that He might reconcile both to God in one body through the cross and put the hostility to death by it. 17 When Christ came, He proclaimed the good news of peace to you who were far away and peace to those who were near. 18 For

through Him we both have access by one Spirit to the Father. [19] So then you are no longer foreigners and strangers, but fellow citizens with the saints, and members of God's household, [20] built on the foundation of the apostles and prophets, with Christ Jesus Himself as the cornerstone. [21] The whole building is being fitted together in Him and is growing into a holy sanctuary in the Lord, [22] in whom you also are being built together for God's dwelling in the Spirit.

He Has Already Done All the Work
Second Corinthians, chapter 5

[1] For we know that if our earthly house, a tent, is destroyed, we have a building from God, a house not made with hands, eternal in the heavens. [2] And, in fact, we groan in this one, longing to put on our house from heaven, [3] since, when we are clothed, we will not be found naked. [4] Indeed, we who are in this tent groan, burdened as we are, because we do not want to be unclothed but clothed, so that mortality may be swallowed up by life. [5] And the One who prepared us for this very thing is God, who gave us the Spirit as a down payment.

[6] Therefore, though we are always confident and know that while we are at home in the body we are away from the Lord— [7] for we walk by faith, not by sight— [8] yet we are confident and satisfied to be out of the body and at home with the Lord. [9] Therefore, whether we are at home or away, we make it our aim to be pleasing to Him. [10] For we must all appear before the judgment seat of Christ, so that each may be repaid for what he has done in the body, whether good or bad.

¹¹ Knowing, then, the fear of the Lord, we persuade people. We are completely open before God, and I hope we are completely open to your consciences as well. ¹² We are not commending ourselves to you again, but giving you an opportunity to be proud of us, so that you may have a reply for those who take pride in the outward appearance rather than in the heart. ¹³ For if we are out of our mind, it is for God; if we have a sound mind, it is for you. ¹⁴ For Christ's love compels us, since we have reached this conclusion: if One died for all, then all died. ¹⁵ And He died for all so that those who live should no longer live for themselves, but for the One who died for them and was raised.

Is There a Better Day Than Today to Say Yes?
Second Corinthians, chapters 5 & 6

¹⁶ From now on, then, we do not know anyone in a purely human way. Even if we have known Christ in a purely human way, yet now we no longer know Him like that. ¹⁷ Therefore if anyone is in Christ, there is a new creation; old things have passed away, and look, new things have come. ¹⁸ Now everything is from God, who reconciled us to Himself through Christ and gave us the ministry of reconciliation: ¹⁹ that is, in Christ, God was reconciling the world to Himself, not counting their trespasses against them, and He has committed the message of reconciliation to us. ²⁰ Therefore, we are ambassadors for Christ; certain that God is appealing through us, we plead on Christ's behalf, "Be reconciled to God." ²¹ He made the One who did not know sin to be sin for us, so that we might become

the righteousness of God in Him.

¹ Working together with Him, we also appeal to you: "Don't receive God's grace in vain." ² For He says:

In an acceptable time, I heard you,
and in the day of salvation, I helped you.

Look, now is the acceptable time; look, now is the day of salvation.

You've Got to Face God Some Day
Hebrews, chapter 4

¹² For the word of God is living and effective and sharper than any two-edged sword, penetrating as far as to divide soul, spirit, joints, and marrow; it is a judge of the ideas and thoughts of the heart. ¹³ No creature is hidden from Him, but all things are naked and exposed to the eyes of Him to whom we must give an account.

Why Not Do It Now?
Hebrews, chapter 4

¹⁴ Therefore since we have a great high priest who has passed through the heavens—Jesus the Son of God—let us hold fast to the confession. ¹⁵ For we do not have a high priest who is unable to sympathize with our weaknesses, but One who has been tested in every way as we are, yet without sin. ¹⁶ Therefore let us approach the throne of grace with boldness, so that we may receive mercy and find grace to help us at the proper time.

THE BOTTOM LINE

Christ Has Already Won the Battle
Colossians, chapter 1

11 May you be strengthened with all power, according to His glorious might, for all endurance and patience, with joy 12 giving thanks to the Father, who has enabled you to share in the saints' inheritance in the light. 13 He has rescued us from the domain of darkness and transferred us into the kingdom of the Son He loves, 14 in whom we have redemption, the forgiveness of sins.

15 He is the image of the invisible God,
the firstborn over all creation;
16 because by Him
everything was created,
in heaven and on earth,
the visible and the invisible,
whether thrones or dominions
or rulers or authorities—
all things have been created through Him and for Him.

17 He is before all things,
and by Him all things hold together.
18 He is also the head of the body, the church;
He is the beginning,
the firstborn from the dead,
so that He might come to have first place in everything.
19 Because all the fullness was pleased to dwell in Him,
20 and to reconcile everything to Himself through Him
by making peace through the blood of His cross—
whether things on earth or things in heaven.

21 And you were once alienated and hostile in mind because of your evil actions. 22 But now He has reconciled you by His physical body through His death, to present you holy, faultless, and blameless before Him— 23 if indeed you remain grounded and steadfast in the faith, and are not shifted away from the hope of the gospel that you heard.

Don't Be Fooled into Thinking He Hasn't
Colossians, chapter 2

4 I am saying this so that no one will deceive you with persuasive arguments. 5 For I may be absent in body, but I am with you in spirit, rejoicing to see your good order and the strength of your faith in Christ.

6 Therefore as you have received Christ Jesus the Lord, walk in Him, 7 rooted and built up in Him and established in the faith, just as you were taught, and overflowing with thankfulness.

8 Be careful that no one takes you captive through philosophy and empty deceit based on human tradition, based

on the elemental forces of the world, and not based on Christ. 9 For in Him the entire fullness of God's nature dwells bodily, 10 and you have been filled by Him, who is the head over every ruler and authority. 11 In Him you were also circumcised with a circumcision not done with hands, by putting off the body of flesh, in the circumcision of the Messiah. 12 Having been buried with Him in baptism, you were also raised with Him through faith in the working of God, who raised Him from the dead. 13 And when you were dead in trespasses and in the uncircumcision of your flesh, He made you alive with Him and forgave us all our trespasses. 14 He erased the certificate of debt, with its obligations, that was against us and opposed to us, and has taken it out of the way by nailing it to the cross.

Let Him Show You What Real Life Looks Like
Romans, chapter 12

1 Therefore, brothers, by the mercies of God, I urge you to present your bodies as a living sacrifice, holy and pleasing to God; this is your spiritual worship. 2 Do not be conformed to this age, but be transformed by the renewing of your mind, so that you may discern what is the good, pleasing, and perfect will of God.

You Won't Be Able to Figure It Out by Yourself
First Corinthians, chapter 1

18 For to those who are perishing the message of the cross is foolishness, but to us who are being saved it is God's power. 19 For it is written:

I will destroy the wisdom of the wise,
and I will set aside the understanding of the experts.

20 Where is the philosopher? Where is the scholar? Where is the debater of this age? Hasn't God made the world's wisdom foolish? 21 For since, in God's wisdom, the world did not know God through wisdom, God was pleased to save those who believe through the foolishness of the message preached. 22 For the Jews ask for signs and the Greeks seek wisdom, 23 but we preach Christ crucified, a stumbling block to the Jews and foolishness to the Gentiles. 24 Yet to those who are called, both Jews and Greeks, Christ is God's power and God's wisdom, 25 because God's foolishness is wiser than human wisdom, and God's weakness is stronger than human strength.

Following Christ Is a Whole New Way of Thinking
First Corinthians, chapter 1

26 Brothers, consider your calling: not many are wise from a human perspective, not many powerful, not many of noble birth. 27 Instead, God has chosen the world's foolish things to shame the wise, and God has chosen the world's weak things to shame the strong. 28 God has chosen the world's insignificant and despised things—the things viewed as nothing—so He might bring to nothing the things that are viewed as something, 29 so that no one can boast in His presence. 30 But from Him you are in Christ Jesus, who for us became wisdom from God, as well as righteousness, sanctification, and redemption, 31 in order

that, as it is written: "The one who boasts must boast in the Lord."

And You Can Trust Him to Take You There
First Corinthians, chapter 2

¹ When I came to you, brothers, announcing the testimony of God to you, I did not come with brilliance of speech or wisdom. ² For I determined to know nothing among you except Jesus Christ and Him crucified. ³ And I was with you in weakness, in fear, and in much trembling. ⁴ My speech and my proclamation were not with persuasive words of wisdom, but with a demonstration of the Spirit and power, ⁵ so that your faith might not be based on men's wisdom but on God's power.

Let's Review

Here Are The Essentials of the Gospel
First Corinthians, chapter 15

¹ Now brothers, I want to clarify for you the gospel I proclaimed to you; you received it and have taken your stand on it. ² You are also saved by it, if you hold to the message I proclaimed to you—unless you believed to no purpose. ³ For I passed on to you as most important what I also received:

> that Christ died for our sins
> according to the Scriptures,
> ⁴ that He was buried,
> that He was raised on the third day
> according to the Scriptures,
> ⁵ and that He appeared to Cephas,
> then to the Twelve.
> ⁶ Then He appeared to over five hundred brothers at one time,
> most of whom remain to the present,
> but some have fallen asleep.
> ⁷ Then He appeared to James,
> then to all the apostles.
> ⁸ Last of all, as to one abnormally born,
> He also appeared to me.

⁹ For I am the least of the apostles, unworthy to be called an apostle, because I persecuted the church of God. ¹⁰ But by God's grace I am what I am, and His grace toward me was not ineffective. However, I worked more than any of them, yet not I, but God's grace that was with me. ¹¹ Therefore, whether it is I or they, so we preach and so you have believed.

Everything Hinges on Christ
First Corinthians, chapter 15

¹² Now if Christ is preached as raised from the dead, how can some of you say, "There is no resurrection of the dead"? ¹³ But if there is no resurrection of the dead, then Christ has not been raised; ¹⁴ and if Christ has not been raised, then our preaching is without foundation, and so is your faith. ¹⁵ In addition, we are found to be false witnesses about God, because we have testified about God that He raised up Christ—whom He did not raise up if in fact the dead are not raised. ¹⁶ For if the dead are not raised, Christ has not been raised. ¹⁷ And if Christ has not been raised, your faith is worthless; you are still in your sins. ¹⁸ Therefore those who have fallen asleep in Christ have also perished. ¹⁹ If we have placed our hope in Christ for this life only, we should be pitied more than anyone.

He Has Conquered Death for Us
First Corinthians, chapter 15

²⁰ But now Christ has been raised from the dead, the firstfruits of those who have fallen asleep. ²¹ For since death came through a man, the resurrection of the dead also comes

through a man. 22 For just as in Adam all die, so also in Christ all will be made alive. 23 But each in his own order: Christ, the firstfruits; afterward, at His coming, the people of Christ. 24 Then comes the end, when He hands over the kingdom to God the Father, when He abolishes all rule and all authority and power. 25 For He must reign until He puts all His enemies under His feet. 26 The last enemy He abolishes is death. 27 For "He has put everything under His feet." But when it says "everything" is put under Him, it is obvious that He who puts everything under Him is the exception. 28 And when everything is subject to Him, then the Son Himself will also be subject to Him who subjected everything to Him, so that God may be all in all.

29 Otherwise what will they do who are being baptized for the dead? If the dead are not raised at all, then why are people baptized for them? 30 Why are we in danger every hour? 31 I affirm by the pride in you that I have in Christ Jesus our Lord: I die every day! 32 If I fought wild animals in Ephesus with only human hope, what good does that do me? If the dead are not raised, "Let us eat and drink, because tomorrow we die." 33 Do not be deceived: "Bad company corrupts good morals." 34 Become right-minded and stop sinning, because some people are ignorant about God. I say this to your shame.

So What Happens After We Die?
First Corinthians, chapter 15

35 But someone will say, "How are the dead raised? What kind of body will they have when they come?" 36

Foolish one! What you sow does not come to life unless it dies. 37 And as for what you sow—you are not sowing the future body, but only a seed, perhaps of wheat or another grain. 38 But God gives it a body as He wants, and to each of the seeds its own body. 39 Not all flesh is the same flesh; there is one flesh for humans, another for animals, another for birds, and another for fish. 40 There are heavenly bodies and earthly bodies, but the splendor of the heavenly bodies is different from that of the earthly ones. 41 There is a splendor of the sun, another of the moon, and another of the stars; for star differs from star in splendor. 42 So it is with the resurrection of the dead:

Sown in corruption, raised in incorruption;
43 sown in dishonor, raised in glory;
sown in weakness, raised in power;
44 sown a natural body, raised a spiritual body.

If there is a natural body, there is also a spiritual body. 45 So it is written: "The first man Adam became a living being"; the last Adam became a life-giving Spirit. 46 However, the spiritual is not first, but the natural; then the spiritual.

47 The first man was from the earth
and made of dust;
the second man is from heaven.
48 Like the man made of dust,
so are those who are made of dust;
like the heavenly man,
so are those who are heavenly.
49 And just as we have borne
the image of the man made of dust,
we will also bear
the image of the heavenly man.

Death Gets Swallowed Up in Life
First Corinthians, chapter 15

50 Brothers, I tell you this: flesh and blood cannot inherit the kingdom of God, and corruption cannot inherit incorruption. 51 Listen! I am telling you a mystery:

We will not all fall asleep,

but we will all be changed,

52 in a moment, in the twinkling of an eye,

at the last trumpet.

For the trumpet will sound,

and the dead will be raised incorruptible,

and we will be changed.

53 Because this corruptible

must be clothed with incorruptibility,

and this mortal

must be clothed with immortality.

54 Now when this corruptible

is clothed with incorruptibility,

and this mortal

is clothed with immortality,

then the saying that is written will take place:

Death has been swallowed up in victory.

55 O Death, where is your victory?

O Death, where is your sting?

56 Now the sting of death is sin,

and the power of sin is the law.

57 But thanks be to God,

who gives us the victory

through our Lord Jesus Christ!

58 Therefore, my dear brothers, be steadfast, immovable, always abounding in the Lord's work, knowing that your labor in the Lord is not in vain.

This Is the Absolute Truth
First John, chapter 5

6 Jesus Christ—He is the One who came by water and blood; not by water only, but by water and by blood. And the Spirit is the One who testifies, because the Spirit is the truth. 7 For there are three that testify: 8 the Spirit, the water, and the blood—and these three are in agreement. 9 If we accept the testimony of men, God's testimony is greater, because it is God's testimony that He has given about His Son. 10 (The one who believes in the Son of God has the testimony in himself. The one who does not believe God has made Him a liar, because he has not believed in the testimony that God has given about His Son.) 11 And this is the testimony: God has given us eternal life, and this life is in His Son.

12 The one who has the Son has life. The one who doesn't have the Son of God does not have life. 13 I have written these things to you who believe in the name of the Son of God, so that you may know that you have eternal life.

This Is What We Know
First John, chapter 5

18 We know that everyone who has been born of God does not sin, but the One who is born of God keeps him,

and the evil one does not touch him.

¹⁹ We know that we are of God, and the whole world is under the sway of the evil one.

²⁰ And we know that the Son of God has come and has given us understanding so that we may know the true One. We are in the true One—that is, in His Son Jesus Christ. He is the true God and eternal life.

We Are Saved by Faith in Jesus Christ Alone
Romans, chapter 10

⁸ᵇ This is the message of faith that we proclaim: ⁹ if you confess with your mouth, "Jesus is Lord," and believe in your heart that God raised Him from the dead, you will be saved. ¹⁰ With the heart one believes, resulting in righteousness, and with the mouth one confesses, resulting in salvation. ¹¹ Now the Scripture says, "No one who believes on Him will be put to shame," ¹² for there is no distinction between Jew and Greek, since the same Lord of all is rich to all who call on Him. ¹³ For "everyone who calls on the name of the Lord will be saved."

To God Be the Glory
Jude

²⁴ Now to Him who is able to protect you from stumbling and to make you stand in the presence of His glory, blameless and with great joy, ²⁵ to the only God our Savior, through Jesus Christ our Lord, be glory, majesty, power, and authority before all time, now, and forever. Amen.